Autism

Louise Spilsbury
Illustrated by Ximena Jeria

Franklin Watts
Published in paperback in Great Britain in 2019 by The Watts Publishing Group

Copyright © The Watts Publishing Group, 2018

Editor: Melanie Palmer
Design: Lisa Peacock and Peter Scoulding
Author: Louise Spilsbury
Consultant: Dr Patricia McNair

ISBN: 978 1 4451 5659 0

Printed in Great Britain by Bell and Bain Ltd, Glasgow

FSC
www.fsc.org

MIX
Paper from
responsible sources
FSC® C104740

Franklin Watts
An imprint of
Hachette Children's Group
Part of The Watts Publishing Group
Carmelite House
50 Victoria Embankment
London EC4Y 0DZ

An Hachette UK Company
www.hachette.co.uk

www.franklinwatts.co.uk

Autism

Questions
and Feelings
About ...

The world is full of different kinds of people.
We all look different on the outside.

How do you look
different to
your friends?

We are all different on the inside, too.
Autism affects the way the brain works.

But every child who has autism is affected in different ways.

Some children with autism find conversations difficult. They may not look at the person they are speaking to. They might be unsure about when to ask or answer questions. Or they may just prefer to avoid other people.

They may find it easier when people show them how to do something rather than just telling them.

People often use words or phrases that have two different meanings. This can be confusing for some people with autism.

'It's raining cats and dogs' sounds silly to people with autism. They don't know it means 'It's raining hard'. They think it actually means that cats and dogs are falling from the sky.

What other phrases have two different meanings?

People often show how they feel by the expression on their face. A smile means they are happy or joking and a frown means they are serious.

What expressions do you use?

If you have autism, it can be hard to know how people feel because you may not spot or understand expressions or signals like these. A big smile might look fierce to you.

If a child with autism laughs when someone falls down, it's not because they think it's funny. They may not realise the person could be hurt or understand why someone cries.

But they can learn about how other people show feelings and when to ask if someone is okay.

Sometimes children with autism can feel uncomfortable or cautious about physical contact with others.

Some children with autism like a hug, but others prefer to shake hands or do a high five instead!

How do you like to show people you care?

Bright lights, loud noises and strong smells can trouble some children with autism. When things get too much, they may feel overwhelmed and shout, hit or push.

They are so upset they don't know what to do.
If people are kind and calm, they feel better soon.

New places and new things can be a challenge for children with autism. They often like things to stay the same or prefer to follow regular routines.

They may like to do things in a certain way. They may like to eat the same things for breakfast at the same time or walk down the same side of a street every day.

What routines do you like to follow?

Many children with autism have a hobby that they like to do a lot. They might be very interested in one thing, and collect lots of facts about it.

Having a hobby is a great thing for everyone.

What hobbies do you have?

At school, everyone is better at some subjects than others. Some children with autism may find it hard to understand stories or poems, where you need to use your imagination. They may be better at maths, computing or learning facts.

What school subjects
are you good at?

Children with autism find the rules of some games hard to follow. They may not know how they are supposed to behave when playing with other people.

They may prefer to do things alongside rather than with other children. They may find it more peaceful.

Do you like playing alone sometimes?

Having autism is just a small part of who a person is. When we get to know people we often find we have a lot in common or like the same things.

What do you do with friends?

We should be proud of the ways we are all
the same and the ways we are all different.
We shouldn't worry about the things that other
people don't like to do, but focus on what we can
do together instead!

Notes for parents and teachers

This book can be a useful way for families and professionals to start a discussion with children about aspects of the autistic spectrum disorder. Autism affects how people communicate and interact socially. It can be hard for other neurotypical children to understand autism because it has no physical signs.

Having autism can be challenging for the individual and those around them. It's important to help neurotypical children to understand what autism is and its effects. For example, knowing why a child who has hyperacute senses might react angrily or violently to a situation, helps others understand and means that they won't take these reactions personally.

Being open and discussing autism can help children to understand that the condition is just one part of a person. None of us should be defined by one thing (like the fact we wear glasses): we are all made up of a variety of thoughts, feelings, likes and dislikes and talents. Learning to accept differences and being able to find things in common with others is an important part of growing up. Doing some activities that focus on participation and inclusivity will help to bridge the differences in a class or group.

Classroom or group activities:

1. Ask children to sit quietly and to think about their surroundings. How it would feel if lights were very much brighter, all the noises were much louder and the smells in the air were much, much stronger? Would it be hard to concentrate on anything else?

2. Hold a session talking about what everyone in the group is good at and thinking about how they can build on or develop those talents. Being positive means thinking about what we can all do rather than what people cannot do.

3. Think about different ways of learning. How do the children think they learn best? Do they like to do things themselves, write things down, watch someone else doing things or have things explained in words?

4. Get the group to trace their handprints onto paper and decorate them with images or words about who they are. Then display the results. This should help them see ways they are similar to and different from the others.

Further Information

Books

I See Things Differently: A First Look at Autism by Pat Thomas and Lesley Harker (Wayland, 2015)

How Are You Feeling Today? by Molly Potter and Sarah Jennings (Featherstone, 2014)

My Brother is Autistic by Jennifer Moore-Mallinos (Barrons, 2008)

We're all Wonders by R J Palacio (Puffin, 2017)

Websites

www.autism.org.uk – The National Autistic Society

www.childautism.org.uk – Support, advice and services for children with autism

www.mencap.org.uk/learning-disability-explained/conditions/autism-and-aspergers-syndrome – A charity supporting people with learning disabilities